LIGHTNING
BOLT
BOOKS™

Mini Horses

Buffy Silverman

Lerner Publications • Minneapolis

Editor's note: A mini horse is typically defined as any small horse that is about 35 inches (89 cm) tall from the bottom of its mane. According to this definition, ponies may be considered mini horses.

Lerner Publications Company
A division of Lerner Publishing Group, Inc.
241 First Avenue North
Minneapolis, MN 55401 USA

For reading levels and more information, look up this title at www.lernerbooks.com.

Library of Congress Cataloging-in-Publication Data

Names: Silverman, Buffy, author.
Title: Mini horses / Buffy Silverman.
Description: Minneapolis : Lerner Publications, [2017] | Series: Lightning bolt books. Little pets | Audience: Ages 6-9. | Audience: K to grade 3. | Includes bibliographical references and index.
Identifiers: LCCN 2017015171 (print) | LCCN 2017024362 (ebook) | ISBN 9781512483079 (eb pdf) | ISBN 9781512483048 (lb : alk. paper)
Subjects: LCSH: Miniature horses—Juvenile literature.
Classification: LCC SF293.M56 (ebook) | LCC SF293.M56 S52 2017 (print) | DDC 636.1/09—dc23
LC record available at https://lccn.loc.gov/2017015171

Manufactured in the United States of America
1-43325-33145-6/5/2017

Table of Contents

Meet the Mini Horse

Imagine leading a tiny horse around town. The horse runs, jumps, and plays. It is a mini horse!

You might be taller than a mini horse!

This horse weighs almost 2,000 pounds (907 kg).

Mini horses look like other horses, but they are much smaller. Adult mini horses usually weigh 150 to 250 pounds (68 to 113 kg). Other horses may weigh 1,800 pounds (816 kg) or more.

People keep mini horses as pets. But mini horses do not live inside a home. They sleep in a shed or a barn. They play and eat in a yard or a pasture.

Mini horses come in many colors. They are white, gray, black, brown, or yellow. Some have small spots or large patches. Mini horses have manes on the backs of their necks.

A Mini Horse is Born

Clomp! Clomp! A mother mini horse walks back and forth. A baby horse has grown inside her for eleven months. The mother lies down and gives birth.

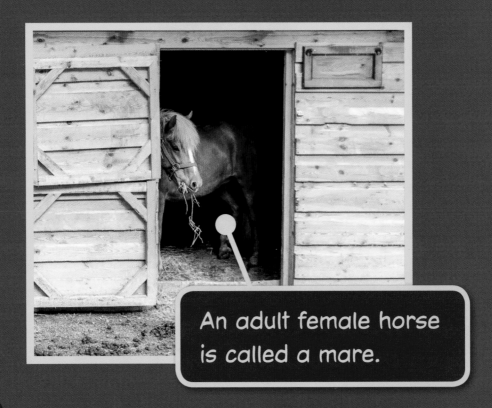

An adult female horse is called a mare.

The new baby stays close to its mother. A baby horse is called a foal. The foal and mare rest. The mare licks her foal clean.

The foal weighs about 20 pounds (9 kg) at birth.

Soon the little foal stands on its long legs. It drinks its mother's milk. The milk has special nutrients to keep the foal healthy.

Mini horses stand within an hour after they are born.

A young foal plays in a pasture.

In a few hours, the foal runs and jumps. It follows the mare. It will stay with its mother for a few months. Then the foal will be ready for a new home.

Mini Horse Life

Mini horses quickly become part of their human families. Foals learn to trust people who handle them gently. Mini horses are usually calm and friendly when people pet them.

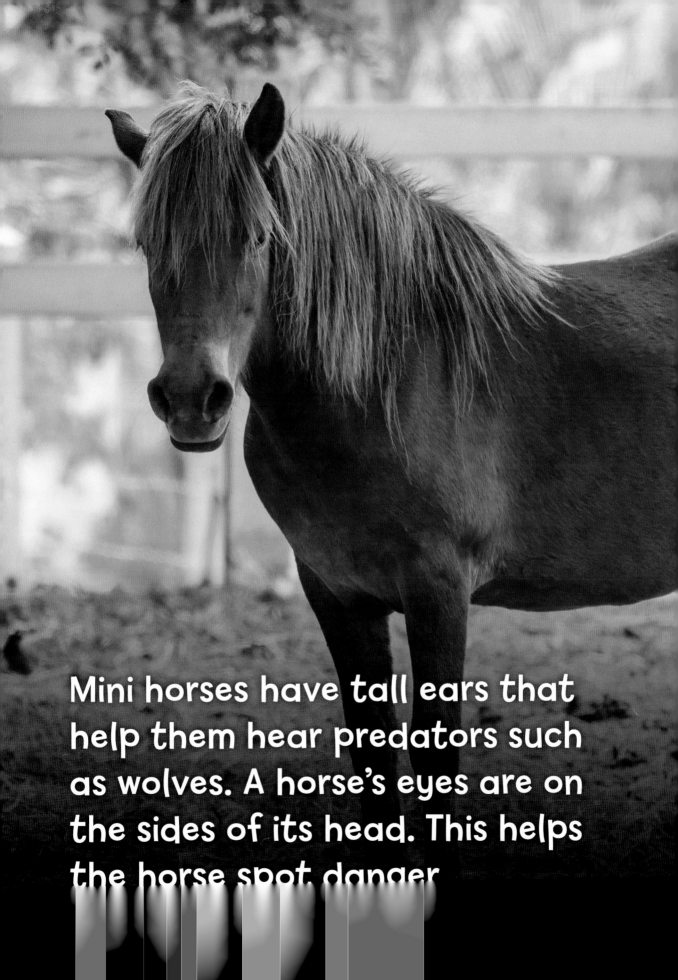

Mini horses have tall ears that help them hear predators such as wolves. A horse's eyes are on the sides of its head. This helps the horse spot danger.

Strong fences keep pet mini horses safe. They spend most of their time eating grass and playing.

14

Mini horses are too small for adults to ride. But they are strong. Mini horses can learn to pull heavy carts.

Caring for a Mini Horse

People who own mini horses care for their pets every day. Horses need plenty of fresh water. Their living space must be cleaned often.

This girl is combing her mini horse.

People feed mini horses at least two times a day. The pets eat 2 to 4 pounds (0.9 to 1.8 kg) of hay each day.

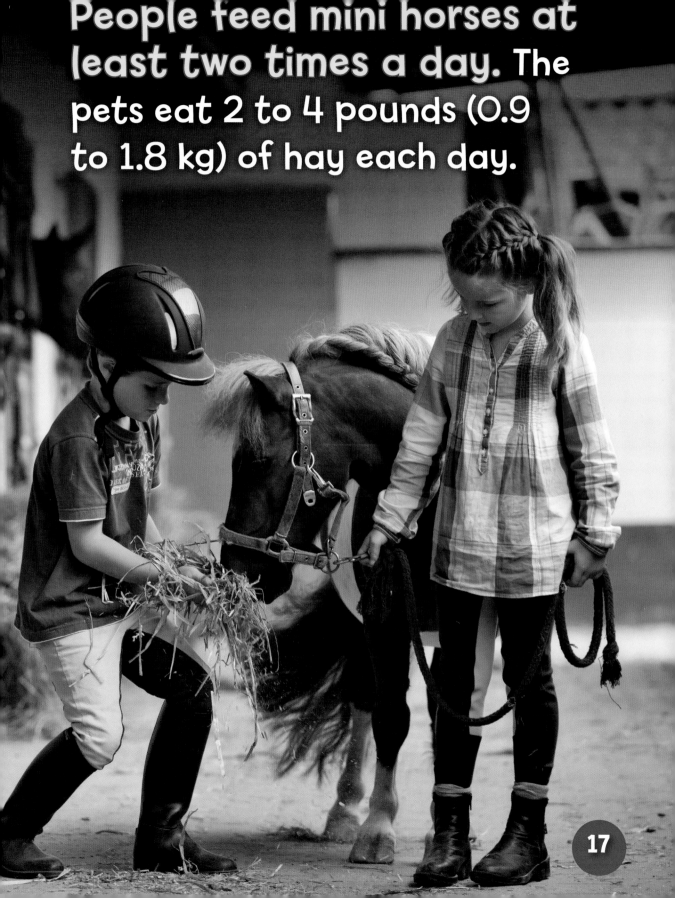

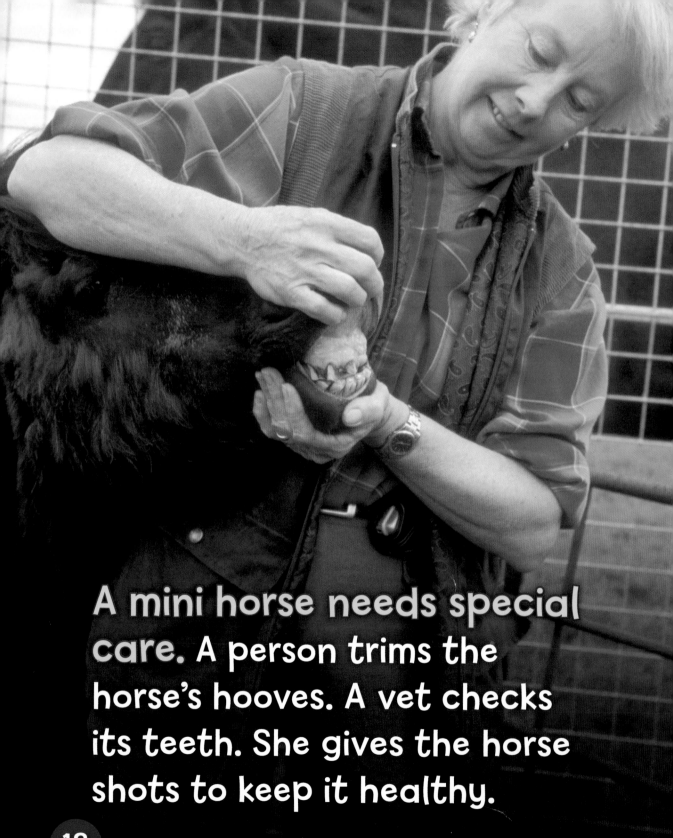

A mini horse needs special care. A person trims the horse's hooves. A vet checks its teeth. She gives the horse shots to keep it healthy.

An owner brushes a mini horse. She cleans its hooves with a special tool. The horse leans into its person and gives a horse hug!

Mini horses live for about thirty years.

Mini Horse Diagram

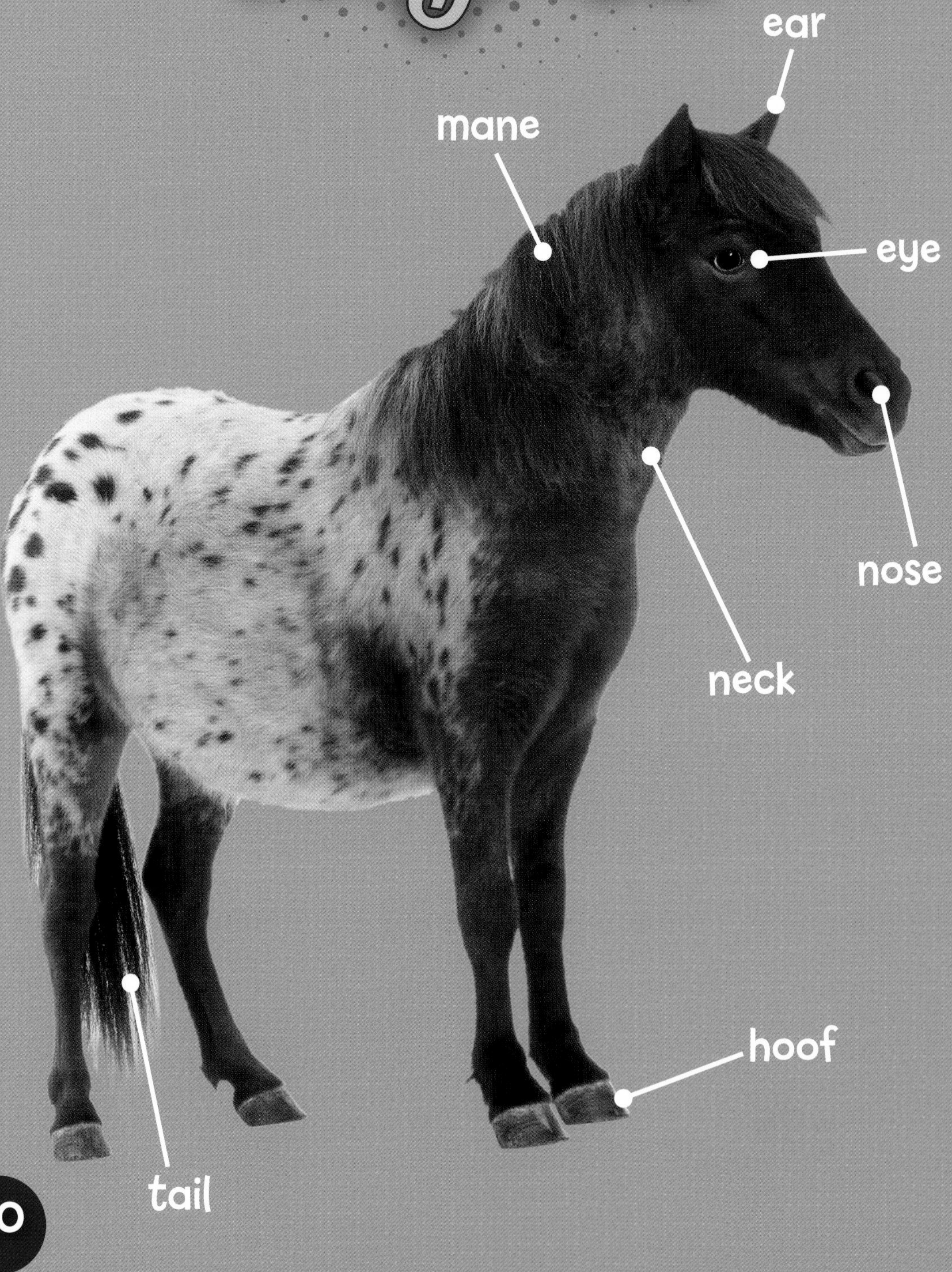

ear

mane

eye

nose

neck

hoof

tail

Fun Facts

- King Louis XIV (the 14th) of France kept mini horses more than 350 years ago. The zoo at his palace had tiny horses and other animals.

- One of the world's smallest horses is named Thumbelina. She weighs just 60 pounds (27 kg). Thumbelina visits sick children in hospitals.

- Mini horses can be trained to help blind people. A guide horse safely leads a person through buildings and along city streets.

Glossary

hoof: a thick covering that protects the foot of a horse. The plural of *hoof* is *hooves*.

mane: long hair on a horse's neck

nutrient: a substance in food that keeps an animal healthy

pasture: land covered with small plants

predator: an animal that eats another animal

vet: a doctor who cares for animals. *Vet* is short for *veterinarian*.

Further Reading

Cantrell, Charlie. *A Friend for Einstein: The Smallest Stallion*. New York: Disney-Hyperion Books, 2011.

Ducksters: Horse
http://www.ducksters.com/animals/horse.php

"Einstein—the Smallest Horse in the World"
https://www.youtube.com/watch?v=6XQtd9cTGFM

Fun Horse Facts for Kids
http://www.sciencekids.co.nz/sciencefacts /animals/horse.html

Silverman, Buffy. *Meet a Baby Horse*. Minneapolis: Lerner Publications, 2017.

Silverstein, Alvin, Virginia Silverstein, and Laura Silverstein Nunn. *Miniature Horses: Cool Pets!* Berkeley Heights, NJ: Enslow, 2012.

Index

Photo Acknowledgments

The images in this book are used with the permission of: thanongsuk harakunno/
Shutterstock.com, p. 2; Vera Zinkova/Shutterstock.com, p. 4; © iStockphoto.com/
Lindsay_Helms, p. 5; © iStockphoto.com/Groomee, p. 6; © iStockphoto.com/dotana,
p. 7; Jure Gasparic/Alamy Stock Photo, p. 8; Marie Charouzova/Shutterstock.com, p. 9;
Tierfotoagentur/Alamy Stock Photo, p. 10; Marie Charouzova/Alamy Stock Photo, p. 11;
Vasyl Syniuk/Shutterstock.com, p. 12; KP Photograph/Shutterstock.com, p. 13; Woraphon
Nusen/Shutterstock.com, p. 14; iStockphoto.com/jtyler, p. 15; GrapeImages/E+/Getty
Images, p. 16; Westend61/Brand X Pictures/Getty Images, p. 17; Angela Hampton Picture
Library/Alamy Stock Photo, p. 18; iStockphoto.com/Asia Images, p. 19; iStockphoto.com/
GlobalP , p. 20; Vera Zinkova/Shutterstock.com, p. 22.

Front Cover: Palo_ok/Shutterstock.com.

Main body text set in Billy Infant regular 28/36. Typeface provided by SparkType.